THE TRANSCONTINENTAL RAILROAD

BY RENA KORB

Editorial Offices: Glenview, Illinois • Parsippany, New Jersey • New York, New York

Sales Offices: Needham, Massachusetts • Duluth, Georgia • Glenview, Illinois
Coppell, Texas • Sacramento, California • Mesa, Arizona

Looking West

On May 10, 1869, people all across the United States had a reason to celebrate. After six long years of difficult labor, the nation's first **transcontinental railroad** was completed. Those who wished to travel across the great expanse of the growing nation could now do so in ten days or less.

Today people have many choices about how to travel from coast to coast. Many choose to fly, which is the fastest way. Others drive their cars, take a bus, or go by train. For most of the 1800s, however, people had only a few ways to travel out west. Some sailed around the tip of South America or to Panama and back up along the Pacific coast. Others journeyed across the Great Plains by covered wagon. These methods of **transportation** took many months, cost a great deal of money, and posed many dangers.

The completion of the transcontinental railroad in 1869 changed the way Americans traveled from coast to coast.

In 1830 the *Tom Thumb* railcar raced a railcar pulled by a horse. The *Tom Thumb* lost, but railroad owners were sure that trains would soon replace horses.

The "Iron Horse"

The history of the railroad, or the "iron horse" as it was called, began in the United States in the 1820s. The first rail lines were built across the East Coast, where most large cities were located at the time. In August 1830 a historic race took place between the *Tom Thumb*, a steam-driven railcar, and a horse-drawn railcar. Although the *Tom Thumb* lost the race when its engine broke, the **engineers** taking part in the race were convinced that the railroad was the wave of the future.

At this time the country was going through a period of growth and change. The United States won the Mexican War in 1848 and gained land from Mexico in the Southwest. In 1849 thousands of people hurried to California to take part in the **gold rush**. California became a state in 1850.

The United States only had about one thousand miles of railroad tracks in 1835. As the country spread west to the Mississippi River and beyond, so did the rail lines. Within twenty-five years, about thirty thousand miles of track crisscrossed the country.

At first, most people thought that the idea of a transcontinental railroad was ridiculous. When the country expanded, though, many people agreed that the United States needed a railroad line that reached to the Pacific Ocean. What they did not agree on was the route that the railroad should take.

In 1853 the government sent engineers to survey, or look over, the land. They studied five possible routes. While leaders in Congress argued about which route was best, a railroad engineer in California named Theodore Judah took action. He charted a new route that followed the trail of the pioneers. He then convinced four California businesspeople to form the Central Pacific Railroad Company in 1861. Known as the "Big Four," these men went to Washington, D.C., and declared that they were ready to start building the first transcontinental railroad.

Leland Stanford was one of the "Big Four." He was a California businessperson and a state governor.

Building the Tracks

Once engineers had chosen the railroad's route, workers cleared the path of trees and stones. Workers then built the roadbed, or the surface for the railroad, on flat land. In the mountains, workers often had to carve a flat piece of land out of rock and steep cliffs.

Once the roadbed was ready, huge groups of workers laid the tracks. First they planted railway crossties, or wooden supporting beams, firmly into the ground. They then placed two long iron rails parallel across the crossties. Finally, they hammered the rails onto the crossties with spikes.

The Transcontinental Railroad

Congress agreed to the plan suggested by the Big Four. In 1862 the Pacific Railway Act was passed. The government gave the Central Pacific the right to lay tracks eastward from Sacramento, California. The government also created a new company, called the Union Pacific Railroad Company, to lay tracks heading westward. The two lines would meet somewhere along the route.

The Central Pacific held a groundbreaking ceremony in January 1863, in Sacramento. Railroad officials made several speeches, and then workers dug their shovels into the ground. The building of the transcontinental railroad had begun!

From the terminal in Sacramento, workers laid tracks through the town and then headed toward the unsettled lands to the east. At first progress was slow, and by September 1865 Central Pacific work crews had constructed only fifty-five miles of track.

Meanwhile, progress on the Union Pacific line went even more slowly. In December 1863 a groundbreaking ceremony took place in Omaha, Nebraska, which had been chosen as the starting point for the rail lines heading west. However, work did not begin until July 1865, a delay mostly due to the Civil War.

This postcard shows the first engine to operate on the Central Pacific Railroad out of Sacramento, California.

The Crew of the Central Pacific

At first the Central Pacific had a hard time finding workers. The work was difficult and dangerous, and many laborers demanded more than thirty-five dollars a month—a lot of money in those days. The company advertised for workers, but those workers who came rarely stayed for long.

By early 1865 only a few hundred Irish **immigrants** had been hired by the Central Pacific. As a possible solution to this problem, the Central Pacific hired fifty Chinese immigrants. The immigrants arrived at the railroad camps in the summer of 1865. At first, the other workers did not welcome them. Many Chinese, however, immediately proved to be skilled, hardworking, and courageous workers.

Soon the Central Pacific hired Chinese immigrants in San Francisco and asked agents in China to send even more workers. By the time the railroad was done, about ten thousand Chinese immigrants had done most of the labor.

About ten thousand Chinese immigrants worked on the transcontinental railroad.

Finding such industrious workers proved to be important. The easiest part of the job had been the miles in and around Sacramento. However, as the tracks drew farther away, the land changed. The railroad tracks soon led into the foothills of the nearby Sierra Nevada. Just ahead stood the most difficult challenge of all: the peaks of Sierra Nevada looming thousands of feet high.

The Challenge of the Sierra Nevada

Working six days a week, crews carved roadbeds out of steep mountainsides, blew up cliffs, cut passages through solid rock, and dug fifteen tunnels through the mountains. At one particularly steep cliff, Chinese workers dangled in reed baskets high above a river to hammer out a roadbed. Because they had no mechanical equipment, workers used picks, shovels, axes, animals, wheelbarrows, and gunpowder to do the work.

During the winter of 1866–1867, snowslides killed dozens of workers.

The crews were drilling tunnels near the top of a mountain pass when the winter of 1866 hit. For the next few months, crews braved freezing temperatures, piles of snow, dozens of storms, and a blizzard that lasted thirteen days. Workers lived in tunnels underneath the snow, or in shacks on the mountainside. Work continued around the clock, but the track advanced only about eight inches a day.

The Union Pacific Heads West

Once the Civil War ended in 1865, work on the Union Pacific took off. From Omaha, crews of former soldiers, freed African Americans, and European immigrants—particularly Irish immigrants—laid tracks westward across the flat prairie.

The problems of the Union Pacific crews were different from those experienced by the Central Pacific workers. Instead of high mountains, the Union Pacific workers faced the Plains Indians. The railroad tracks ran through their hunting grounds. This is where the Plains Indians trapped the buffalo that provided them with food, fur, and almost everything they needed to live. Work on the railroad scared away the buffalo, and some workers even shot the animals for sport. The Plains Indians tried to keep the train away by attacking the crews. Soldiers, however, were sent to guard the crews and the tracks continued to move westward.

The Race to the Finish

In 1868 the Central Pacific line came down from the Sierra Nevada. With both companies now on flat land, workers rushed to complete the most track—and to earn as much money as possible. The railroad companies, however, had never set a meeting point for the two sets of tracks. By the spring of 1869, each company had cleared roadbeds that did not connect, but ran past each other, missing one another by more than one hundred miles.

President Andrew Johnson and Congress forced officials from the two companies to meet and find a solution. Officials chose a spot where the miles of railroad tracks would finally join: Promontory, Utah. On April 9, 1869, a competition began. The crews of each company wanted to be the first to reach Promontory. This race captured the attention of people all over the country. They eagerly followed the railroad's progress, mile by mile, in the newspapers.

The race also inspired the crews from both companies to work at top speed. Central Pacific workers laid six miles of track in a single day. Then Union Pacific crews laid seven miles of track in a single day. On April 28, working from sunup until seven o'clock at night, a Central Pacific crew set a record by completing more than ten miles of track. Two days later the Central Pacific crews reached Promontory and laid down their tools. They had won the race to the finish.

The First Transcontinental Railroad, 1869

The transcontinental railroad made a trip across the country much quicker and more comfortable.

The Opening of the Railroad

One day after the Central Pacific crews reached Promontory, the crews of the Union Pacific drew within sight of their goal. The transcontinental railroad stood at the brink of completion. The two railroad companies had built 1,776 miles of track in six years.

The two railroad companies planned a grand celebration at Promontory to honor the project's completion. On May 10, 1869, Leland Stanford, the president of the Central Pacific Railroad, strode up to the rails in front of a crowd of spectators, reporters, and special guests. Using a silver hammer, he swung at a specially made solid gold spike—and missed. Then Dr. Thomas C. Durant, head of the Union Pacific Railroad, took a try. He missed too. A few moments later, a railway worker drove in the last spike. A cheer went up from the crowd, and the amazing news was announced: "Done!" People around the country joined in the celebration with speeches, parades, and bell ringing.

Traveling West

The transcontinental railroad opened up the country. Each week tourists, travel reporters, and job seekers boarded a train starting in the East and traveled to the West in comfort. During the journey, which lasted for eight to ten days, passengers could sleep in comfortable berths, or built-in beds, eat in the dining cars, and purchase candy and magazines.

The transcontinental railroad was just the first of several railroads that would eventually cross the continent. Additional trains soon connected communities all over the nation. The United States had at last fulfilled its hope of spreading from coast to coast.

Glossary

engineer a person who uses scientific and mathematical ideas to design, make, and run structures and machines

gold rush the sudden movement of many people to an area where gold has been found

immigrant a person who comes to live in a new land

transcontinental railroad a railroad that crosses a continent

transportation the moving of goods, people, or animals from one place to another

THE
TRANSCONTINENTAL
RAILROAD

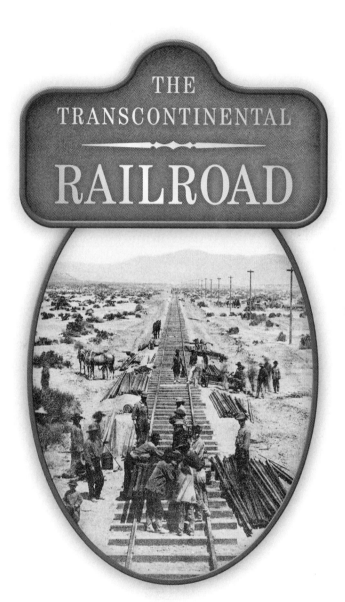

BY **RENA KORB**

Editorial Offices: Glenview, Illinois • Parsippany, New Jersey • New York, New York

Sales Offices: Needham, Massachusetts • Duluth, Georgia • Glenview, Illinois
Coppell, Texas • Sacramento, California • Mesa, Arizona

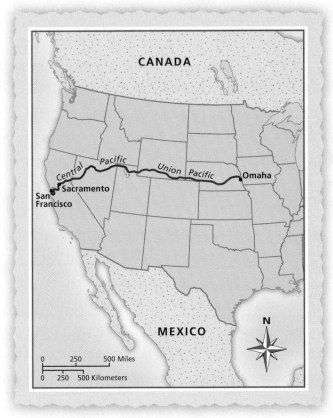

THE TRANSCONTINENTAL
RAILROAD

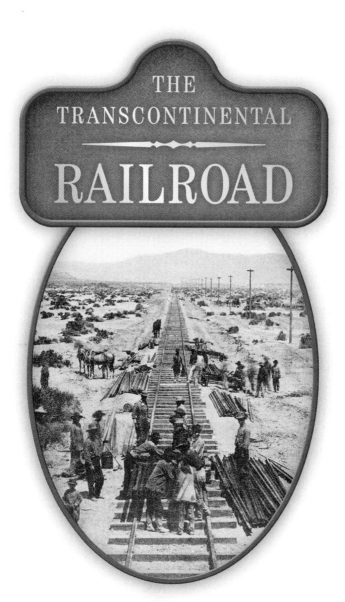

BY RENA KORB

PEARSON
Scott
Foresman

Editorial Offices: Glenview, Illinois • Parsippany, New Jersey • New York, New York

Sales Offices: Needham, Massachusetts • Duluth, Georgia • Glenview, Illinois
Coppell, Texas • Sacramento, California • Mesa, Arizona